A Spring Harvest

by

GEOFFREY BACHE SMITH

COMPASS CIRCLE

A Spring Harvest.
Current edition published by Compass Circle in 2020.

Published by Compass Circle
Cover copyright ©2020 by Compass Circle.

Note:
All efforts have been made to preserve original spellings and punctuation of the original edition which may include old-fashioned English spellings of words and archaic variants.

This book is a product of its time and does not reflect the same views on race, gender, sexuality, ethnicity, and interpersonal relations as it would if it were written today.

For information contact :
information@compass-circle.com

But even as he spoke, the hand of God
Worked on the sombre branches, and straightway
They were all green with sap, and bud, and leaf,
As at the very bidding of the spring

GEOFFREY BACHE SMITH

SECRET WISDOM OF THE AGES SERIES

Life presents itself, it advances in a fast way. Life indeed never stops. It never stops until the end. The most diverse questions peek and fade in our minds. Sometimes we seek for answers. Sometimes we just let time go by.

The book you have now in your hands has been waiting to be discovered by you. This book may reveal the answers to some of your questions.

Books are friends. Friends who are always by your side and who can give you great ideas, advice or just comfort your soul.

A great book can make you see things in your soul that you have not yet discovered, make you see things in your soul that you were not aware of.

Great books can change your life for the better. They can make you understand fascinating theories, give you new ideas, inspire you to undertake new challenges or to walk along new paths.

Classics like the one of Geoffrey Bach Smith are indeed a secret to many, but for those of us lucky enough to have discovered them, by one way or another, these books can enlighten us. They can open a wide range of possibilities to us. Because achieving greatness requires knowledge.

The series SECRET WISDOM OF THE AGES presented by Compass Circle try to bring you the great timeless masterpieces of personal development, positive thinking, and the law of attraction.

We welcome you to discover with us fascinating works by Socrates, Plato, Henry Thoreau, among others.

Contents

NOTE

T HE poems of this book were written at very various times, one ("Wind over the Sea") I believe even as early as 1910, but the order in which they are here given is not chronological beyond the fact that the third part contains only poems written after the outbreak of the war. Of these some were written in England (at Oxford in particular), some in Wales and very many during a year in France from November 1915 to December 1916, which was broken by one leave in the middle of May.

"The Burial of Sophocles," which is here placed at the end, was begun before the war and continued at odd times and in various circumstances afterwards; the final version was sent me from the trenches.

Beyond these few facts no prelude and no *envoi* is needed other than those here printed as their author left them.

J. R. R. T.

1918.

If there be one among the Muses nine
Loves not so much *Completion* as *the Will,*
And less the austere saint than the fond sinner:
Loves scanty ruins, garlanded with years,
Better than lofty palaces entire:
To her I dedicate this spoiléd sheaf
Of rime that scarcely came to harvesting.

There is a window here in Magdalen
Composite, methinks, of fragments that stark Mars
Has scattered. Even so my verses be
Composite of memories and half-uttered dreams
Welded together sans due ordinance,
Which might have been far other, but that Mars
Scattered and harried them with his ruthless flail.

I

TWO LEGENDS

Glastonbury

Thither through moaning woods came Bedivere,
At gloomy breaking of a winter's day,
Weary and travel-stained and sick at heart,
With a great wound gotten in that last fray
Ere he stood by, and watched the King depart
Down the long, silent reaches of the mere:
And all the earth was sad, and skies were drear,
And the wind cried, and chased the relict leaves
Like ships, that the storm-tossed ocean batters and heaves,
And they fly before the gale, and the mariners fear.

So he found at the last an hermitage
Hard by a little hill, and sheltering trees
That bent gaunt branches in the winter's breeze;
And he drew rein, and leant, and struck the door:
Then presently came forth an hermit sage
And helped him to dismount with labour sore:
Straight went they in, but Bedivere being lame
Stumbled against the open door, and swooned,
And would have fallen, but the hermit caught
And laid him gently down; then hurrying brought
From a great chest a cordial, and came
That he might drink, and so beheld his wound.

Long time lay Bedivere betwixt life and death,

Like a torn traveller on a stormy height

'Twixt one wind and another: till his breath

Came easier, and he prospered. Then did sleep

Bathe him in soothing waters, soft and deep,

And left him whole, at breaking of the light,

So he beheld the old man, and desired

That he would tell of whom he was, and whence.

Whereat once more the ancient eyes were fired:

"I, I was Arthur's bishop, at his court

And in his church I ministered, and thence

When at the last the whole was overthrown

With wrath and ill designings, straight I sought

A place where I might die, too feeble grown

To endure a new beginning to my years

When once the past was lost, and whelmed in tears.

Hither I came, where, in the dawns of time

Dim peoples, that the very stones forget,

Lived, loved, and fought, and wove the riddling rime

On a lake island mystically set.

They passed, and after ages manifold

Came wandering sainted Joseph (even he

That tended God's frail body, and enrolled

In linen clothes of spicèd fragrancy).

He brought the vessel, vanished now from earth

That wrought destruction to the Table Round,

Since many deemed themselves above their worth

4

And sought in vain, and perished ere they found."

Then Bedivere: "Alas the King! I saw
The unstayed overwhelming tide of war:
And when the opposèd standards were unfurled
Of Arthur and of Mordred, his base son,
Ere yet the noise of battle was begun
I heard the heralds crying to the world:

"'Ye that have sought out pallid harmonies
Where never wind blows, save the gentle south:
Ye that have trafficked on the sounding seas
And fear nor cheerless rains, nor scorching drouth:

"'Ye that have piled the rich, full-ripened crops
Of word and measure, till the rime, grown proud,
Did straight contemn the leaping mountain tops
And lose itself in air, and riven cloud:

"'Ye that have lived a dangerous life of war
Whose speech has been bold words and heady boasts
Gather, for strife and death unknown before,
Come gather all unto the fronting hosts.'

"I saw the last dim battle in the mist
There, where a dreary waste of barren sand
Doth mark the ultimate leagues of this fair land;
Scarce we beheld the foe we struck, or wist

Which party had advantage: like thin wraiths
Fit to throng Lethe banks the warriors
Struck and o'ercame, or fell, unseen, unwept;
And alien hopes, lives, peoples, alien faiths
Were all confounded on those desolate shores.
And ever the mist seethed, and the waves kept
A hollow chanting, as they mourned the end
Of all mankind, and of created time.
How many fell therein of foe or friend
I know not, save that when the darkness came
And the mist cleared, I found at last the King,
His armour and visage fouled with blood and slime,
And fading in his eyes the ancient flame.

"I saw him make on Mordred with his spear,
And crying 'Tide me death, betide me life,
He shall not live, that wrought the accursed thing,'
Put a dread ending to the outworn strife.
I saw them fall together, and, drawn near.
Knew that the King was wounded unto death.

"Then as he drew with growing pain his breath
I looked, and saw a long, black barge that stole
Across the waters, like a wandering soul
Returnèd from the woeful realm, to view
The ancient haunts well-loved that once it knew.
And when it touched the shallows I did bear
The dying Arthur as he bade, and there

6

I placed him 'mid dark forms: I could not tell
Whose they might be; and wept, and breathed farewell."

Then spake the eremite: "Beyond yon door
There stands a chapel, ancient and weatherworn,
And there did worship in the days of yore
The sons of kings. The night ere you came hither
I was awakened by the sound of feet.
And I looked forth, and saw a body borne
By veilèd figures straight, as they knew whither,
In at the chapel gateway. I went down
And found that they had digged a grave, most meet
For one of saintly life, or king by birth:
They seemed some score, and by blown candles' light
I saw that each with tears bedewed his gown
Ere sank the corse into the waiting earth,
Then prayed, and so went out into the night."

Thereon the twain arose, and went straightway
Toward the old, dim chapel, and beheld
The stone beneath whose length the body lay:
Kneeling they closely scanned it all, and spelled
Graven in golden character, "Arcturus
Rex Quondamque Futurus."

Quoth Bedivere:
"Thank God this voice remaineth unto us;
Now I do mind me of a prophecy

7

Spoken long since in some emblazoned year,
How Arthur should escape mortality
And lie beneath the hills, in cavern deep
Or on some shore, where faery seas do break:
Around him all his warriors shall sleep,
Who at a great bell's sounding shall awake
What time th' old enemy spreads death and harm
Thorough his ancient realm, and the last woes
Go over her; his own victorious arm
Shall rid the stricken land of hate and foes."

So leave we them, each head inaureoled
With the awakening spring's young sunlight-gold.

Then, on an evening, hurrying footsteps rung
Without the door, and straight 'twas open flung,
They saw who stood therein, and each one knew
The face unspared by years and strife and shame,
Pale as the moon is pale on winter nights,
With deep eyes dreaming like September haze,
Or lit with lust of battle, eyes that few
Had looked on and forgot; in such wise came
Lancelot, the hero of immortal fights,
Lancelot, the golden knight of golden days.

"Whence cam'st thou, Lancelot?" "Even from the
    Queen,
The Queen that was, whom now a convent's shade

8

Imprisons, and a dark and tristful veil
Enwraps those brows, that in old days were seen
Most puissant proud of all that ever made
The traitor honest, and the valorous frail.

"Yet evermore about her form there clings
And evermore shall cling, the ancient grace,
Like evening sunlight lingering on the mere:
And till the end of all created things
There shall be some one found, shall strive to trace
The immortal loveliness of Guinevere.

"Shall I not mind me of old ecstasies
In Camelot, beneath the ancient walls,
In shady paths, and marble terraces
Rose-fragrant, where eternal sunlight falls.
But ah! the last long kiss is ta'en and given,
And the last look in those unfathomed eyes,
The passionate last embrace is coldly riven,
And all is grief, beneath the pitiless skies.

"Gods of the burnt-out hearth, the wandered wind,
Gods of pale dawns that vanished long ago,
Gods of the barren tree, the withered leaf.
The faded flower, and the ungarnered sheaf,
Gods half-forgot in the wild ages' flow
Yours, yours am I, that all for nought have sinned."

Spring, summer passed away, and autumn rain
Swelled the lean brooks, until the gelid year
Shot forth its icy hand, and grasped again.
Again the hanging clouds were struck and furled
By winds of winter, until skies were clear,
And there was frost o' nights, and all the world
Lay glistening to the newly risen sun.

Till came that season, wherein solemn days
Do celebrate the reign on earth begun
Of the most blessèd Child, whenas all ways
Were bound, and all the fields were white with snow.
Then in the chapel at high noon they three
Offered their quiet orisons and so
Came forth and looked upon the purity,
And when he saw the fields all stainless-white
Lancelot groaned in spirit, and spake: "How sore
And no wise joyous to a sinner's sight
Is this dear land, where the snow lies untrod.
Even so once before the eyes of God
My soul lay all unspotted; now no more."

"Courage, my son, and patience," quoth the sage;
No sin there is, that shall not lose its stain
Through the great love of God, and His dear Son.
Repent and be forgiven: know that none
Shall sue before His throne, and sue in vain,
Nor shall one name be blotted from the page

If he that bears it turn to prayer and tears."

Then Lancelot: "Though through the tale of years
That still are left before the longed-for earth
Receive my body, I should strive amain
To slay myself, and gain regenerate birth,
Alas it were all profitless and vain.
Verily, when I came unto this place
I railed on God, that I had lost my soul
And nothing gained: until a heavenly grace
Enwrapped me, like some sick man made half whole,
And now my grief is only for old sin.
But ah, what boots it? Lo, this barren tree
(He touched a shrub that grew beside the door),
This tree, methinks, shall bud and blossom before
I pass the gates divine, and enter in
To the fair country I must never see."

But even as he spoke, the hand of God
Worked on the sombre branches, and straightway
They were all green with sap, and bud, and leaf,
As at the very bidding of the spring,
Burst forth, and soon each tender branch was gay
With flowers that nodded in the winter's breeze
(So blossomed in old time the prophet's rod),
And Lancelot stood and saw the wondrous thing.

Then softly spake the hermit, "Now is grief

Reproved, and sorrow cast out with the lees;

For God beholds the living, not the dead;

And He that took the semblance of a child

Loves He but penance, and the drooping head,

Has He not sung for joy, has He not smiled?"

So they grew old together, and the years

Pressed no more to their lips the cup of tears

(They had drained all, maybe). And ever less

Seemed all things mortal, as in quietness

They pondered the eternal mysteries

(The noblest heritage of all men born),

Such as are writ upon the face of dawn,

Or in the glamour of a moonlit night,

Or in the autumn swallow's southern flight,

Or in the breaking of the restless seas:

Or dreamed rich, hallowed dreams of aureate days

While yet the King was young, and sunlight fell

On bower and roof of ancient Camelot:

Of triumph clarion, and thanksgiving bell,

When all was song, and laughter, and high praise,

Even when as yet the accursed thing was not.

Then would loom out from the chill mists of time

The faces and the forms remembered still,

The King and Guinevere, and Galahad,

That rode upon a peerless quest and dire,

Kay, swift and hasty as a flame of fire,

And gentle Percival, whom to give made glad;
Merlin, contriver of the riddling rime,
And Gawain, silent harbinger of ill.

So as the day draws ever toward the dark,
Ever toward peace the great wind's sounding breath,
And ever toward the further shore the bark
They drew to the dark, silent realm of death.

Far, far away from their old palace-halls
Where once they lived a splendid life and vain,
That now are scattered stones and crumbled walls
In some soft vale, or by the echoing main,

Beneath the springing grass, and very deep
They three do lie, where never mornings rise
To ope the portals of their dazèd eyes,
Nor ever mortal footstep breaks their sleep,

And near beside lies Arthur, even he
That was King once, and yet again shall be.

Legend

Grey, ancient abbeys, you may see them yet,

In that high plain above the western sea:

A broken arch or two, a few worn stones

Piled one upon another, and for paving

Uneven fragments with tall grass between:

Grass that is always green, winter and summer,

The grass that grows on long-forgotten graves.

It was a springtime morning long ago,

A morning of blue skies and whitest clouds,

And singing birds, and singing streams, and woods

That shone like silver, yet untouched with green:

The brethren of an abbey of the plain

—Whereof what now is ruin yet was whole—

Were labouring as holy brethren must,

Quietly, and in peace: and elder ones

Paced in the cloister, and some, older still,

Too old to work or dream, sat in the sunlight,

The sunlight which they soon should see no more.

And there came from the wood upon the hill

One clothed in the sere habit of a monk,

That passed in at the portal of the abbey:

Brighter his face than is the face of spring,

And joy was in his tread, as in his soul.

And some that paced the cloister paused to glance at him,

And one that went upon an errand stayed,

And some that laboured left their work, and came

Gathering round him, and he spake, and said:

"Very fair the golden morning
　　As in yonder wood I strayed,
And I heard diviner music
　　Than the greatest harpers made,

For a sweet bird sang before me
　　Songs of laughter, and of tears.
All that I have loved and longed for,
　　As I measured out my years.

Sang of blessed shores and golden
　　Where the old, dim heroes be,
Distant isles of sunset glory,
　　Set beyond the western sea.

Sang of Christ and Mary Mother
　　Hearkening unto angels seven
Playing on their golden harp-strings
　　In the far courts of high Heaven."

So they stood by, and listened to his speech,

Rhythmic, for that great joy was in his soul:
But while they wondered whence he was, and who,
He cast his eyes around, and, shuddering, cried:
"Who are ye, that I thought to be my brothers?
Strangers and sons of strangers! Where are they
I left behind me but an hour ago?"
Then was there whispering among the throng,
And wonder not a little, and some scorn;
Till he that spake, with anguish in his eye,
Cried: "Take me to a cell, that I may pray."
'Twas done, and in the golden afternoon
A brother entered, and found none within,
Only a sere monk's habit, and much dust,
As of a body crumbled in the grave.

And while they wondered what these things might be,
At last spake forth the oldest of them all,
Burdened with hundred winters in his soul:
"I can remember, when my years were young,
Hearing the old monks say, one went from here
When spring was on the earth, as it is now,
Some five-score years ago, and was not seen
Again, though search was made in all the land."

And some believed this was the same, and all
Forgot it in a sennight's silent toil.
Save one, that saw, and seeing understood,
And for the greater glory of High God

16

Wrote down the story in a mighty book,

And limned the old saint hearkening to the bird

With bright hues, and you still may read and see.

II
FIRST POEMS

Rime

O scholar grey, with quiet eyes,
Reading the charactered pages, bright
With one tall candle's flickering light,
In a turret chamber under the skies;
O scholar, learned in gramarye,
Have you seen the manifold things I see?

Have you seen the forms of tracèd towers
Whence clamorous voices challenge the hours:
Gaunt tree-branches, pitchy black
Against the long, wind-driven wrack
Of scurrying, shuddering clouds, that race
Ever across the pale moon's face?

Have you heard the tramp of hurrying feet.
There beneath, in the shadowy street,
Have you heard sharp cries, and seen the flame
Of silvery steel, in a perilous game,
A perilous game for men to play,
Hid from the searching eyes of day?

Have you heard the great awakening breath,
Like trump that summons the saints from death,
Of the wild, majestical wind, which blows

18

Loud and splendid, that each man knows

Far, O far away is the sea,

Breaking, murmuring, stark and free?

All these things I hear and see,

I, a scholar of gramarye:

All are writ in the ancient books

Clear, exactly, and he that looks

Finds the night and the changing sea,

The years gone by, and the years to be:

(He that searches, with tireless eyes

In a turret-chamber under the skies)

Passion and joy, and sorrow and laughter,

Life and death, and the things thereafter.

To an Elzevir Cicero

Dust-covered book, that very few men know,

   Even as very few men understand

   The glory of an ancient, storied land

In the wild current of the ages' flow,

Have not old scholars, centuries ago

   Caressed you in the hollow of their hand,

   The while with quiet, kindly eyes they scanned

Your pages, yellowed now, then white as snow?

A voice there is, cries through your every word,

Of him, that after greatest glory came

   Down the grey road to darkness and to tears;

A voice like far seas in still valleys heard,

Crying of love and death and hope and fame

    That change not with the changing of the years.

To a Dürer Drawing of Antwerp Harbour

Figured by Dürer's magic hand wast thou,

    That, lightning-like, traced on the lucid page

    Rough, careless lines, with wizardry so sage

That yet the whole was fair, I know not how:

Ships of gaunt masts, and stark, sea-smitten prow,

    Idle, yet soon again to sweep the main

    In the swift service of old merchants' gain,

Where are ye now, alas, where are ye now?

Gone are ye all, and vanished very long,

    Sunk with great glory in the storied wars,

      Or conquered by the leaping breakers wild:

And yet we love your image, like some song

    That tells of ancient days and high, because

      Old Dürer looked upon you once and smiled.

Pure Virginia

York River Returns

Like smoke that vanishes on the morning breeze

    Are passed the first beginnings of the world,

    When time was even as a bud still curled,

And scarce the limit set of lands and seas;

Like smoke, like smoke the composite auguries

    Of Hebrew and of Hellene are all furled,

20

Fulfilled or else forgot, and idly hurled

This way or that way, as the great winds please:

Aye, and like smoke of this delicious herb

    Brought by strange ways the curious mind may guess,

      From where the parrot and the leopard be,

My thoughts, that should be strong, the years to curb

    Go up, and vanish into nothingness

      On a blue cloud of exquisite fragrancy.

A Preface for a Tale I have never told

Herein is nought of windy citadels

Where proud kings dwell, that with an iron hand

Deal war or justice: here no history

Of valiant ships upon the wine-dark seas

Passing strange lands and threading channels strait

Between embalmed islands: here no song

That men shall sing in battle and remember

When they are old and grey beside the fire:

Only a story gathered from the hills

And the wind crying of forgotten days,

A story that shall whisper, "All things change—

For friends do grow indifferent, and loves

Die like a dream at morning: bitterness

Is the sure heritage of all men born,

And he alone sees truly, who looks out

From some huge aery peak, considering not

Fast-walled cities, or the works of men,

But turns his gaze unto the mountain-tops

21

And the unfathomable blue of heaven
That only change not with the changing years"———
A tale that shod itself with ancient shoon
And wrapped its cloak, and wandered from the west.

A Sonnet

There is a wind that takes the heart of a man,
    A fresh wind in the latter days of spring,
    When hate and war and every evil thing
That the wide arches of high Heaven span
Seems dust, and less to be accounted than
    The omened touches of a passing wing:
    When Destiny, that calls himself a king,
Goes all forgotten for the song of Pan:
For why? Because the twittering of birds
    Is the best music that was ever sung,
Because the voice of trees finds better words
    Than ever poet from his heartstrings wrung:
Because all wisdom and all gramarye
Are writ in fields, O very plain to see.

"It was all in the Black Countree"

It was all in the Black Countree,
What time the sweet o' the year should be,
I saw a tree, all gaunt and grey,
As mindful of a winter's day:
And that a lonely bird did sit
Upon the topmost branch of it,

22

Who to my thought did sweeter sing
Than any minstrel of a king.

To a Pianist

When others' fingers touch the keys
Then most doleful threnodies
Chase about the air, and run
Like Pandæmonium begun.
Rhythm strained and false accord
In a ceaseless stream are poured;
Then sighs are heard, and men depart
To seek the sage physician's art,
Or silence, and a little ease,
When others' fingers touch the keys.
When your fingers touch the keys

Hark, soft sounds of summer seas
In a melody most fair
Whisper through the pleasant air,
Or a winding mountain stream
Glitters to the pale moonbeam,
Or a breeze doth stir the tops
Of springtime larches in a copse,
Or the winds are loosed and hurled
About the wonder-stricken world
With immortal harmonies,
When your fingers touch the keys.

A Fragment

And some came down in a great wind
  Under grey scurrying skies
To where the long wave-beaten shore
  For ever shrieks and cries.

O, fling aside your toil, your care,
  When one cries of the sea,
And the great waves that foam and toss,
  And the white clouds that flee:
Let us forget our weariness,
  Forget that we have sinned,
So we but sail, what matters it
  If Death ride on the wind?

Storm from the sky, storm from the sea
  Beat on them as they stood,
And a great longing sprang in them
  To cross the roaring flood. . . .

Sea Poppies

'Twixt lonely lands and desert beach,
Where no wind blows and no waves reach,
A sunken precinct here we keep,
With woven wiles of endless sleep;
Our twisted stems of sere-hued green,

Our pallid blooms what sun has seen?
And he that tastes our magic breath
Shall sleep that sleep whose name is death.

Wild clouds are scurrying overhead,
The wild wind's voice is loud and dread,
Sounding the knell of the dying day,
Yet here is silence and gloom alway.
And a great longing seizes me
To burst my bondage and be free,
To look on winds' and waters' strife,
And breathe in my nostrils the breath of life.
Give me not dim and slumbrous ease,
But sounding storm and labouring seas,
Not peaceful and untroubled years,
But toil and warfare and passion and tears.
And I would fall in valorous fight,
And lie on lofty far-seen height.

Yet how to burst these prison-bands,
Forged by unseen spirit-hands?

O seek not to burst our prison bands
Forged by unseen spirit-hands.
Clashing battle and labouring sea,
    These be for others, not for thee.
Thou lover of storm and passion and war
Break'st our charmed circle never more.

"O, sing me a Song of the Wild West Wind"

O, sing me a song of the wild west wind,
 And his great sea-harrying flail,
Of hardy mariners, copper skinned,
 That fly with a bursting sail.
They see the clouds of crispèd white
 That shadow the distant hills,
And filled are they with a strange delight
 As shaking away old ills.

O, give me a boat that is sure and stark,
 And swift as a slinger's stone,
With a sail of canvas bronzèd dark,
 And I will go out alone:
Nor fear nor sorrow my soul shall keep
 When around me lies the sea,
And I will return with the night, and sleep
 In the wind's wild harmony.

Ære Perennius

Written on Commemoration Sunday, Corpus Christi College, Oxford

We praise, we praise the immortal dead,
 Who strove beneath unheeding skies
For truth that raised the drooping head,
 For light that gladdened weary eyes:

26

The martyr's cross, the warrior's sword,
    How should they be of lesser worth
Than some unprofitable hoard
    In ancient mines below the earth?

The song that one alone has sung,
    The great uncompromising page,
Are these but glittering baubles, flung
    About the world from age to age?

But ruin'd columns, wondrous tall,
    Built in old time with labour sore,
The mighty deeds done once for all,
    The voice heard once, and heard no more?

Rather they shine as doth the star
    About the close of winter's day,
That cheers the traveller afar
    And draws him on, and points the way.

We praise, we praise the immortal dead.
    Do they not verily wait till we
Of the spoilt years unharvested
    Be also of their company?

The Old Kings

Far away from sunny rills,
Far away from golden broom,
Far away from any town
Whither merchants travel down—
In a hollow of the hills
In impenetrable gloom
Sit the old forgotten kings
Unto whom no poet sings,
Unto whom none makes bequest,
Unto whom no kingdoms rest,——
Only wayward shreds of dreams,
And the sound of ancient streams,
And the shock of ancient strife
On the further shore of life.

When our days are done, shall we
Enter their pale company?

"O there be Kings whose Treasuries"

O there be kings whose treasuries
   Are rich with pearls and gold
And silks and bales of cramasy
   And spices manifold:
Gardens they have with marble stairs
   And streams than life more fair,
With roses set and lavender

That do enchant the air.

O there be many ships that sail
   The sea-ways wide and blue,
And there be master-mariners
   To sail them straight and true:
And there be many women fair
   Who watch out anxiously,
And are enamoured of the day
   Their dear ones come from sea:

But riches I can find enow
   All in a barren land,
Where sombre lakes shine wondrously
   With rocks on either hand:
And I can find enow of love
   Up there, alone, alone,
With none beside me save the wind,
   Nor speech except his moan.

For there far up among the hills
   The great storms come and go
In a most proud processional
   Of cloud and rain and snow:
There light and darkness only are
   A changing benison
Of the old gods who wrought the world
   And shaped the moon and sun.

A Study

In chamber hung with white,
Lit by the dawning light,

Upon a slender bed
She lies, as she were dead:

Most carven-ivory fair,
And palely gold her hair.

Lo, the sun's yellow ray,
That, with the rise of day,

Through quartered casement came
To wake her life's pale flame.

The Eremite

When the world is still in the hush of dawn,
And yet fast sleeping are hate and scorn,
From my grey lodging under the hill
I do go out, and wander at will.

Of nights when the riven clouds are hurled,
And strife and rancour possess the world,
I sit alone, with thoughts that are chill,
In my grey lodging under the hill.

The House of Eld

Now the old winds are wild about the house,
  And the old ghosts cry to me from the air
Of a far isle set in the western sea,
  And of the evening sunlight lingering there.

Ah! I am bound here, bound and fettered,
  The dark house crumbles, and the woods decay,
I was too fain of life, that bound me here;
  Away, old long-loved ghosts, away, away!

The South-west Wind

The south-west wind has blown his fill,
  And vanished with departing day:
The air is warm, and very still,
  And soft as silks of far Cathay.

This is a night when spirits stray.
  Their wan limbs bear them where they will;
They wring their pallid hands alway,
  Seeing the lights upon the hill.

Schumann: Erstes Verlust

O, dreary fall the leaves,

The withered leaves;

Among the trees

Complains the breeze,

That still bereaves.

All silent lies the mere,

The silver mere,

In saddest wise

Reflecting skies

Forlorn and sere.

Would autumn had not claimed its own

And would the swallows had not flown.

Skies overcast!

Leaves falling fast!

And she has passed

And left the woodland strown,

The woodland strown,

The silver mere,

The dying year,

And me alone.

Skies overcast!

Leaves falling fast!

Does she that passed
Dream of the woodland strown,
The woodland strown,
The silver mere,
The dying year,
And me alone?

"Dark Boughs against a Golden Sky"

Dark boughs against a golden sky,
    And crying of the winter wind:
And sweet it is, for hope is high,
    And sad it is, for we have sinned.

Perfect is nature's every part
    In sunny rest, or windy strife:
But never yet the perfect heart,
    And never yet the perfect life!

Dark boughs against a golden sky,
    And crying of the winter wind:
And in the cold earth we must lie,
    What matter then if we have sinned?

For evermore and evermore
    Shall the great river onward roll:
And ever winding streams and poor
    Shall lose them in the mighty whole.

"Wind of the Darkness"

Wind of the darkness, breathing round us,
   Wind from the never-resting sea,
Lo, you have loosed the cords that bound us,
   Lo, you have set our spirits free:

Free to take wings, like the sea-bird lonely
   Beating hardily up the wind:
Fixed are his eyes on the waters only,
   Never a glance for the land behind.

Wind of the darkness, breathing round us,
   Wind from the never-resting sea.
Was it the old gods' voice that found us
   Here, where the bars of prison be?

From the far isle that neither knoweth
   Change of season, nor time's increase,
Where is plenty, and no man soweth:
   Calling to strife that shall end in peace.

Creator Spiritus

The wind that scatters dying leaves
   And whirls them from the autumn tree
Is grateful to the ship that cleaves
   With stately prow the scurrying sea.

Heedless about the world we play
  Like children in a garden close:
A postern bars the outward way
  And what's beyond it no man knows:

For careless days, a life at will,
  A little laughter, and some tears,
These are sufficiency to fill
  The early, vain, untroubled years,

Till at the last the wind upheaves
  His unimagined strength, and we
Are scattered far, like autumn leaves,
  Or proudly sail, like ships at sea.

Wind over the Sea

Only a grey sea, and a long grey shore,
And the grey heavens brooding over them.
Twilight of hopes and purposes forgot,
Twilight of ceaseless eld, and when was youth?
Is it not lonely here, beyond the years?

Out of the gathering darkness crashes a wind from the
  ocean,
Rushing with league-long paces over the plain of the
  waters,
Driving the clouds and the breakers before it in sudden
  commotion.

Who are these on the wind, riders and riderless horses?

Riders the great ones that have been and are, and those
    to come shall be:

These are the children of might, life's champions and
    history's forces.

Might I but grasp at a bridle, and fear not to be trodden
    under,

Swing myself into a saddle, and ride on greatly, exulting

On down the long straight road of the wind, a galloping
    thunder!

Only a grey sea, and a long grey shore,

And the grey heavens brooding over them,

Twilight of hopes and purposes forgot,

Twilight of ceaseless eld, for when was youth?

Is it not lonely here, beyond the years?

Songs on the Downs

1

This is the road the Romans made,
    This track half lost in the green hills,
Or fading in a forest-glade
    'Mid violets and daffodils.

The years have fallen like dead leaves,

    Unwept, uncounted, and unstayed

(Such as the autumn tempest thieves),

    Since first this road the Romans made.

2

A miser lives within this house,

His patron saint's the gnawing mouse,

And there's no peace upon his brows.

A many ancient trees and thin

Do fold the place their shade within,

And moan, as for remembered sin.

III

LAST POEMS AND "THE BURIAL OF SOPHOCLES"

"We who have bowed ourselves to Time"

We who have bowed ourselves to time
Now arm an uneventful rime
   With panoply of flowers
   Through the long summer hours. . . .

But now our fierce and warlike Muse
Doth soft companionship refuse,
   And we must mount and ride
   Upon a steed untried. . . .

We who have led by gradual ways
Our placid life to sterner days
   And for old quiet things
   Have set the strife of kings,

Who battled have with bloody hands
Through evil times in barren lands,
   To whom the voice of guns
   Speaks and no longer stuns,

Calm, though with death encompassèd,
That watch the hours go overhead
   Knowing too well we must

With all men come to dust. . . .

Crave of our masters' clemency
Silence a little space that we
   Upon their ear may force
   Tales of our trodden course.

Anglia Valida in Senectute

(On the Declaration of War)

Not like to those who find untrodden ways;
   But down the weary paths we know,
Through every change of sky and change of days
   Silent, processional we go.

Not unto us the soft, unlaboured breath
   Of children's hopes and children's fears:
We are not sworn to battle to the death
   With all the wrongs of all the years:

We are old, we are old, and worn and school'd with ills,
   Maybe our road is almost done,
Maybe we are drawn near unto the hills
   Where rest is and the setting sun:

But yet a pride is ours that will not brook
   The taunts of fools too saucy grown,
He that is rash to prove it, let him look
   He kindle not a fire unknown.

Since first we flung our gauntlet to the skies
　　And dared the high Gods' will to bend,
A fire that still may burn deceit and lies
　　Burn and consume them to the end.

"Dark is the World our Fathers left us"

Dark is the world our fathers left us,
　　Wearily, greyly the long years flow,
Almost the gloom has of hope bereft us,
　　Far is the high gods' song and low:

Sombre the crests of the mountains lonely,
　　Leafless, wind-ridden, moan the trees:
Down in the valleys is twilight only,
　　Twilight over the mourning seas:

Time was when earth was always golden,
　　Time was when skies were always clear:
Spirits and souls of the heroes olden,
　　Faint are cries from the darkness, hear!

Tear ye the veil of time asunder
　　Tear the veil, 'tis the gods' command,
Hear we the sun-stricken breakers thunder
　　Over the shore where the heroes stand.

Dark is the world our fathers left us,
  Heavily, greyly the long years flow,
Almost the gloom has of hope bereft us,
  Far is the high gods' song and low.

Awakening

Gold-crested towers against the veilèd skies,
Sere branches of the winter trees beneath,
And a low song, and heavy-lidded eyes;

Is there aught else in all the world beside?
Is not time stilled and ended in this hour?

———

Up, and away! the belted squadrons ride!

Ave atque Vale

In Oxford, evermore the same
  Unto the uttermost verge of time,
Though grave-dust choke the sons of men,
  And silence wait upon the rime,

At evening now the skies set forth
  Last glories of the dying year:
The wind gives chase to relict leaves:
  And we, we may not linger here.

A little while, and we are gone:
   God knows if it be ours to see
Again the earliest hoar-frost white
   On the long lawns of Trinity.

In Merton, of the many courts
   And doorways good to wander through,
Gable and spire shall glitter white
   Or tawny gold against the blue:

And still the winter sun shall smile
   At noonday, or at sunset hour
On Magdalen, girt with ancient trees,
   Beneath her bright immortal tower.

Though nevermore we tread the ways
   That our returning feet have known
Past Oriel, and Christ Church gate
   Unto those dearer walls, our own.

———

Oxford is evermore the same,
   Unto the uttermost verge of time,
Though grave-dust choke the sons of men,
   And silence wait upon the rime.

"O, one came down from Seven Hills"

O, one came down from seven hills
  And crossèd seven streams:
All in his hands were thyme and grass
  And in his eyes were dreams:
He passèd by a seven fields
  With early dews all grey
And entered in the stricken town
  About the break of day.

"O you old men that stand and talk
  About the market-place,
There is much trouble in your eyes
  And anguish in your face:
O woman in a silent room
  Within a silent house,
There is no pleasure in your voice
  Or peace upon your brows."

"O how should such as we rejoice
  Who weep that others die,
Who quake, and curse ourselves, and watch
  The vengeful hours go by?
O better far to fly the grief
  That wounds, and never kills;
O better far to fly the town
  And seek the seven hills——"

"I will go pray the seven gods
    Who keep the seven hills
That they do grant your city peace,
    And easement of her ills."
"Nay, rather pray the seven gods
    To launch the latest pain;
For there be many things to do
    Ere we see peace again."

"Then I'll go praise the seven gods
    With hymns and chauntings seven,
Such as shall split the mountain-tops
    And shrivel up blue heaven:
That there be men who mock at threats
    And wag their heads at strife,
Love home above their own hearts' blood
    And honour more than life."

Sonnet to the British Navy

Lest force aspire to brand an alien name
    Upon the immortal empire of the free:
Lest fire and sword and slaughter strive to tame
    This isle, was ne'er so tamed, and ne'er shall be.
Ye guard the ocean barrier, undismayed
    'Midst hidden perils for a brave man's fears,
In iron craft that many smiths have made
    With peaceful labour in the old, dead years.

In a small vessel, of one Smith ill-wrought
  I must soon venture on another deep,
And dare, with little hope, and little thought
  Of praise and honour and untroubled sleep:
So, as each sails upon his perilous sea,
  I pray High God He strengthen you, and me.

The Last Meeting

We who are young, and have caught the splendour of
    life,
  Hunting it down the forested ways of the world,
Do we not wear our hearts like a banner unfurled
  (Crowned with a chaplet of love, shod with the sandals
    of strife)?

Now not a lustre of pain, nor an ocean of tears
  Nor pangs of death, nor any other thing
That the old tristful gods on our heads may bring
  Can rob us of this one hour in the midst of the years.

The New Age and the Old

Like the small source of a smooth-flowing river,
  Like the pale dawn of a wonderful day,
Comes the New Age, from High God, the good giver,
  Comes with the shouts of the children at play:

As an old leaf whirls faster and faster
  From the sere branch that once gave it fair birth,

Into the arms of the devil, its master,
    Be the old age swept away from the earth!

To the Cultured

Sons of culture, God-given,
First offspring of Heaven,
Athletic and tanned,
Well-built and not nervous,
With your golf and your tweeds
And your "noble editions,"
Quiet lives and few needs
(Say a thousand a year
For your earthly career)
Who can't understand
Discontent and seditions,
May Heaven preserve us
From being like you.

What are we, what am I?
Poor rough creatures, whose life
Is "depressing" and "grey,"
Is a heart-breaking strife
With death and with shame
And your polite laughter,
Till—the world pass away
In smoke and in flame,
And some of us die,
And some live on after
To build it anew.

Afterwards

Afterwards, when
The old Gods' hate
On the riven earth
No more is poured:

When weapons of war
Are all outworn
What shall become
Of the race of men?

One shall go forth
In the likeness of a child:
Under sere skies
Of a grey dawning:

One shall go forth
In the likeness of a child,
And desolate places
Shall spring and blossom:

One shall go forth
In the likeness of a child:
And men shall sing
And greatly rejoice:

All men shall sing

For the love that is in them,

And he shall behold it

And sing also.

Domum redit Poeta

O much desired from far away

   And long, I hold thee once again,

Thou undiminished treasury

   Of small delights, yet nowise vain:

The cat curled on the cosy hearth,

   The thrushes in the garden trees,

The memories of younger years,

   The quiet voices, and the peace.

Memories

Shapes in the mist, it is long since I saw you,

   Pale hands and faces, and quiet eyes,

Crowned with a garland the dead years wrought you

   Out of remembrance that never dies:

One among you is tall and supple

   Good to fight or to love beside,

Only the stain of a deadly quarrel,

   Only that and the years divide:

One there is with a face as honest,

   Heart as true, as the open sea,

One who never betrayed a comrade—
   Death stands now betwixt him and me.

One I loved with a passionate longing
   Born of worship and fierce despair,
Dreamed that Heaven were only happy
   If at length I should find him there.

Shapes in the mist, ye see me lonely,
   Lonely and sad in the dim firelight:
How far now to the last of all battles?
   (Listen, the guns are loud to-night!)

Whatever comes, I will strike once surely,
   Once because of an ancient tryst,
Once for love of your dear dead faces
   Ere I come unto you, Shapes in the mist.

Intercessional

There is a place where voices
   Of great guns do not come,
Where rifle, mine, and mortar
   For evermore are dumb:
Where there is only silence,
   And peace eternal and rest,
Set somewhere in the quiet isles
   Beyond Death's starry West.

49

O God, the God of battles,
   To us who intercede,
Give only strength to follow
   Until there's no more need,
And grant us at that ending
   Of the unkindly quest
To come unto the quiet isles
   Beyond Death's starry West.

April 1916

Now spring is come upon the hills in France,
And all the trees are delicately fair,
As heeding not the great guns' voice, by chance
Brought down the valley on a wandering air:
Now day by day upon the uplands bare
Do gentle, toiling horses draw the plough,
And birds sing often in the orchards where
Spring wantons it with blossoms on her brow—
Aye! but there is no peace in England now.

O little isle amid unquiet seas,
Though grisly messengers knock on many doors,
Though there be many storms among your trees
And all your banners rent with ancient wars;
Yet such a grace and majesty are yours
There be still some, whose glad heart suffereth
All hate can bring from her misgotten stores,
Telling themselves, so England's self draw breath,
That's all the happiness on this side death.

"Over the Hills and Hollows Green"

Over the hills and hollows green
   The springtide air goes valiantly,
Where many sainted singing larks
   And blessed primaveras be:

But bitterly the springtide air
   Over the desert towns doth blow,
About whose torn and shattered streets
   No more shall children's footsteps go.

Sonnet

To-night the world is but a prison house,
And kindly ways, and all the springing grass
Are dungeon stones to him that may not pass
Among them, save with anguish on his brows:
And any wretched husbandman that ploughs
The upland acres in his habit spare
Is king, to those in palaces of glass
Who sit with grief and weariness for spouse.

O God, who madest first the world that we
Might happy live, and praise its pleasantness
In such wise as the angels never could,
Wherefore are hearts, fashioned so wondrously,
All spoiled and changed by human bitterness
Into the likenesses of stone and wood?

"O Long the Fiends of War shall dance"

O long the fiends of war shall dance

Upon the stricken fields of France:

And long and long their grisly cry

Shall echo up and smite the sky:

O long and long the tears of God

Shall fall upon a barren sod,

Save when, of His great clemency,

He gives men's hearts in custody

Of grim old kindly Death, who knows

The mould is better than the rose.

For R. Q. G.

July 1916

O God, whose great inscrutable purposes

(Seen only of the one all-seeing eye)

Are as unchangeable as the azure sky,

And as fulfilled of infinite mysteries:

Are like a fast-locked castle without keys

Whereof the gates are very strong and high,

Impenetrable, and we poor fools die

Nor even know what thing beyond them is:

O God, by whom men's lives are multiplied,

Are scattered broadcast in the world like grain,

And after long time reaped again and stored,

O Thou who only canst be glorified

By man's own passion and the supreme pain,

Accept this sacrifice of blood outpoured.

"Sun and Shadow and Winds of Spring"

Sun and shadow and winds of spring,
    Love and laughter and hope and fame,
Cloud and storm-light over the hills,
    Tears and passion and sordid shame:

All, all are but as quenchèd fire
    And vanish'd smoke to him that lies
Amid the silence of the trees
    Under the silence of the skies.

"Let us tell Quiet Stories of Kind Eyes"

Let us tell quiet stories of kind eyes
    And placid brows where peace and learning sate:
Of misty gardens under evening skies
    Where four would walk of old, with steps sedate.

Let's have no word of all the sweat and blood,
    Of all the noise and strife and dust and smoke
(We who have seen Death surging like a flood,
    Wave upon wave, that leaped and raced and broke).

Or let's sit silently, we three together,
    Around a wide hearth-fire that's glowing red,
Giving no thought to all the stormy weather
    That flies above the roof-tree overhead.

And he, the fourth, that lies all silently
    In some far-distant and untended grave,
Under the shadow of a shattered tree,
    Shall leave the company of the hapless brave,

And draw nigh unto us for memory's sake,
    Because a look, a word, a deed, a friend,
Are bound with cords that never a man may break,
    Unto his heart for ever, until the end.

"Save that Poetic Fire"

Save that poetic fire
    Burns in the hidden heart,
Save that the full-voiced choir
    Sings in a place apart,

Man that's of woman born,
    With all his imaginings,
Were less than the dew of morn,
    Less than the least of things.

The Burial of Sophocles

The First Verses

Gather great store of roses, crimson-red
    From ancient gardens under summer skies:
New opened buds, and some that soon must shed
    Their leaves to earth, that all expectant lies;
Some from the paths of poets' wandering,

Some from the places where young lovers meet,

Some from the seats of dreamers pondering,

And all most richly red, and honey-sweet.

For in the splendour of the afternoon,

When sunshine lingers on the glittering town

And glorifies the temples wondrous-hewn

All set about it like a deathless crown,

We will go mingle with the solemn throng,

With neither eyes that weep, nor hearts that bleed,

That to his grave with slow, majestic song

Bears down the latest of the godlike seed.

Many a singer lies on distant isle

Beneath the canopy of changing sky:

Around them waves innumerable smile,

And o'er their head the restless seabirds cry:

But we will lay him far from sound of seas,

Far from the jutting crags' unhopeful gloom,

Where there blows never wind save summer breeze,

And where the growing rose may clasp his tomb.

And thither in the splendid nights of spring,

When stars in legions over heaven are flung,

Shall come the ancient gods, all wondering

Why he sings not that had so richly sung:

There Heracles with peaceful foot shall press

The springing herbage, and Hephæstus strong,

Hera and Aphrodite's loveliness,
   And the great giver of the choric song.

And thither, after weary pilgrimage,
   From unknown lands beyond the hoary wave,
Shall travellers through every coming age
   Approach to pluck a blossom from his grave:
Some in the flush of youth, or in the prime,
   Whose life is still as heapèd gold to spend,
And some who have drunk deep of grief and time,
   And who yet linger half-afraid the end.

The Interlude

It was upon a night of spring,
Even the time when first do sing
The new-returnèd nightingales;
Whenas all hills and woods and dales
Are resonant with melody
Of songs that die not, but shall be
Unto the latest hour of time
Beyond the life of word or rime—
Whenas all brooks more softly flow
Remembering lovers long ago
That stood upon their banks and vowed,
And love was with them like a cloud:
There came one out of Athens town
In a spun robe, with sandals brown,
Just when the white ship of the moon

56

Had first set sail, and many a rune
Was written in the argent stars;
His feet were set towards the hills
Because he knew that there the rills
Ran down like jewels, and fairy cars
Galloped, maybe, among the dells,
And airy sprites wove fitful spells
Of gossamer and cold moonshine
Which do most mistily entwine:
And ever the hills called, and a voice
Cried: "Soon, maybe, comes thy choice
Twixt mortal immortality
Such as shall never be again,
'Twixt the most passionate-pleasant pain
And all the quiet, barren joys
That old men prate about to boys."

He wandered many nights and days—
Whose morns were always crystal clear,
As lay the world in still amaze
Enchanted of the springing year,
And all the nights with wakeful eyes
Watched for another dawn to rise—
Till at the last the mountain tops
Received him, which like giant props
Stand, lest the all-encircling sky
Fall down, and men be crushed and die.

And so he reached a curvèd hill
Whereon the hornèd moon did seem
Her richest radiance to spill
In an inestimable stream,
Like jewels rare of countless price,
Or wizard magic turned to ice.

And as he reached the topmost crest of it,
Lo! the Olympian majesties did sit
In a most high and passionless conclave:
They ate ambrosia with their deathless lips,
And ever and anon the golden wave
Flowed of the drink divine, which only strips
This mortal frame of its mortality.
And there, and there was Aphrodite, she
That is more lovely than the golden dawn
And from a ripple of the sea was born:
And there was Hera, the imperious queen,
And Dian's chastity, that hunts unseen
What time with spring the woodland boughs are green:
And there was Pan with mirth and pleasantness,
And Eros' self that never knew distress
Save for the love of the fair Cretan maid;
There Hermes with the wings of speed arrayed,
And awful Zeus, the king of gods and men,
And ever at his feet Apollo sang
A measure of changing harmonies that rang

From that high mountain over all the world,

And all the sails of fighting ships were furled,

And men drew breath, and there was peace again.

But him that saw, the sight like flame

Or depths of waters overcame:

He swooned, nor heard how ceased the choir

Of strings upon Apollo's lyre,

Nor saw he how the sweet god stood

And smiled on him in kindly mood,

And stooped, and kissed him as he lay;

Then lightly rose and turned away

To join the bright immortal throng

And make for them another song.

The Last Verses

O ageless nonpareil of stars

    That shinest through a mist of cloud,

O light beyond the prison bars

    Remote, unwavering, and proud;

Fortunate star and happy light,

Ye benison the gloom of night.

All hail, unfailing eye and hand,

    All hail, all hail, unsilenced voice,

That makest dead men understand,

    The very dead in graves rejoice:

Whose utterance, writ in ancient books,

Shall always live, for him that looks.

Many as leaves from autumn trees
   The years shall flutter from on high,
And with their multiple decease
   The souls of men shall fall and die,
Yet, while the empires turn to dust,
You shall live on, because you must.

O seven times happy he that dies
   After the splendid harvest-tide,
When strong barns shield from winter skies
   The grain that's rightly stored inside:
There death shall scatter no more tears
Than o'er the falling of the years:

Aye, happy seven times is he
   Who enters not the silent doors
Before his time, but tenderly
   Death beckons unto him, because
There's rest within for weary feet
Now all the journey is complete.

"So we lay down the Pen"

So we lay down the pen,
So we forbear the building of the rime,
And bid our hearts be steel for times and a time
   Till ends the strife, and then,
When the New Age is verily begun,
God grant that we may do the things undone.

Made in the USA
Monee, IL
29 January 2023

26644220R00042